W9-CGX-200

The MIDDLE ROAD: AMERICAN POLITICS

1945–2000

The MIDDLE ROAD: AMERICAN POLITICS

1945–2000

Library
Hogg Middle School
Houston, TX

Christopher Collier
James Lincoln Collier

BENCHMARK BOOKS

MARSHALL CAVENDISH
NEW YORK

ACKNOWLEDGMENT: The authors wish to thank James T. Patterson, Professor of History, Brown University, for his careful reading of the text of this volume of The Drama of American History and his thoughtful and useful comments. The work has been much improved by Professor Patterson's notes. The authors are deeply in his debt, but, of course, assume full responsibility for the substance of the work, including any errors that may appear.

Photo research by James Lincoln Collier
COVER PHOTO: Corbis Bettman
PICTURE CREDITS: Independence National Historic Park: 10; Corbis/Bettman: 15, 18, 20, 21, 25, 27, 28, 30, 31, 34, 35, 36, 39, 42, 43, 44, 45, 50, 51, 54, 56, 57, 62, 64, 65, 69, 70, 71, 72, 76, 79, 81, 85; Author's collection: 84.

Benchmark Books
Marshall Cavendish Corporation
99 White Plains Road
Tarrytown, New York 10591-9001

©2002 Christopher Collier and James Lincoln Collier

All rights reserved. No part of this book may be reproduced or utilized in any form or by any means electronic or mechanical, including photocopying, recording, or by any information storage and retrieval system, without permission from the copyright holders.

Library of Congress Cataloging-in-Publication Data

Collier, Christopher, 1930–
The middle road: American politics, 1945 to 2000 / by Christopher Collier and James Lincoln Collier.
p. cm. – (Drama of American history)
Includes bibliographical references (p.) and index.
ISBN 0-7614-1318-9
1. United States—Politics and government—1945-1989—Juvenile literature.
2. United States—Politics and government—1989-1993—Juvenile literature.
3. United States—Politics and government—1993-2001—Juvenile literature.
[1. United States—History—1945– 2. United States—Politics and government.]
I. Collier, James Lincoln, 1928– II. Title

E743.C588 2001
973.92—dc21   2001025615

Printed in Italy
1 3 5 6 4 2

CONTENTS

Over many years of both teaching and writing for students at all levels, from grammar school to graduate school, it has been borne in on us that many, if not most, American history textbooks suffer from trying to include everything of any moment in the history of the nation. Students become lost in a swamp of factual information, and as a consequence lose track of how those facts fit together and why they are significant and relevant to the world today.

In this series, our effort has been to strip the vast amount of available detail down to a central core. Our aim is to draw in bold strokes, providing enough information, but no more than is necessary, to bring out the basic themes of the American story, and what they mean to us now. We believe that it is surely more important for students to grasp the underlying concepts and ideas that emerge from the movement of history, than to memorize an array of facts and figures.

The difference between this series and many standard texts lies in what has been left out. We are convinced that students will better remember the important themes if they are not buried under a heap of names, dates, and places.

In this sense, our primary goal is what might be called citizenship education. We think it is critically important for America as a nation and Americans as individuals to understand the origins and workings of the public institutions that are central to American society. We have asked ourselves again and again what is most important for citizens of our democracy to know so they can most effectively make the system work for them and the nation. For this reason, we have focused on political and institutional history, leaving social and cultural history less well developed.

This series is divided into volumes that move chronologically through the American story. Each is built around a single topic, such as the Pilgrims, the Constitutional Convention, or immigration. Each volume has been written so that it can stand alone, for students who wish to research a given topic. As a consequence, in many cases material from previous volumes is repeated, usually in abbreviated form, to set the topic in its historical context. That is to say, students of the Constitutional Convention must be given some idea of relations with England, and why the Revolution was fought, even though the material was covered in detail in a previous volume. Readers should find that each volume tells an entire story that can be read with or without reference to other volumes.

Despite our belief that it is of the first importance to outline sharply basic concepts and generalizations, we have not neglected the great dramas of American history. The stories that will hold the attention of students are here, and we believe they will help the concepts they illustrate to stick in their minds. We think, for example, that knowing of Abraham Baldwin's brave and dramatic decision to vote with the small states at the Constitutional Convention will bring alive the Connecticut Compromise, out of which grew the American Senate.

Each of these volumes has been read by esteemed specialists in its particular topic; we have benefited from their comments.

CHAPTER I

A New President Confronts the Peace

The United States, ever since the presidency of George Washington, has run under a "two-party system." Although there were other parties in earlier days, for nearly a hundred and fifty years American politics have been dominated by Republicans and Democrats. This arrangement seems so natural to Americans that they sometimes forget that in dictatorships there is usually only one party, and in some other nations many parties compete for power. The two-party system is not laid out in the Constitution. It exists simply because of some basic differences between political leaders of the founding era like Alexander Hamilton and Thomas Jefferson, and because third parties have never drawn many voters. As a consequence, the political history of the United States in the period we are looking at, from the end of World War II in 1945 to the year 2000, has been basically a contest between Republicans and Democrats. At times one party has prevailed, at times the other; but neither party has been able to really take command except for short periods.

Even the people who belong to the same party do not always agree with each other. At times there is much scrapping within a party over which policies to follow. This was especially the case during the period

The Founding Fathers hated the idea of political parties, which they considered devisive. However, different ideas about government, in particular those held by Alexander Hamilton (left) and Thomas Jefferson (right), inevitably led to contention, and eventually the formation of parties.

of about 1933 to the 1970s when the Democratic Party was divided between northerners who favored activist government with power moving from the states to Washington and state rights southerners who wanted as little interference from the national government as possible. In Congress these southerners often voted with Republicans. During much of the era we are discussing, the Republicans were also divided into liberal and conservative wings. Nonetheless, over the last half century the parties have broadly followed consistent philosophies of government. Generally speaking, since the 1930s the Democrats have favored an active role for government in the American economy and society. They initiated widespread Social Security benefits, government medical programs, and laws protecting the rights of blacks, immigrants, women, and others they see as in need of aid or protection. Many Democrats want strong controls on guns and commercial uses of the environment. They also favor certain restrictions on business and industry so that consumers are fairly treated. The government, they believe, should be a countervailing force to check the power of the great corporations. Finally, Democrats favor relatively high taxes on the well-to-do and the rich.

The Republicans in modern times have tried to shrink big government and reduce the size of the bureaucracy. They want the minimum of regulation of business, and only the most necessary social programs. They believe in what has been called the "trickle down" economic theory. According to this theory, which goes back to George Washington's treasury secretary, if taxes are kept low for the wealthy, the wealthy will pile up money which they can then invest in new businesses or in expanding old businesses. This in turn will provide more jobs and higher levels of living for everybody. However, if taxes are to be kept low, there have to be fewer, less expensive social programs.

The Republicans also believe that the capitalist, free-enterprise system works best if it is allowed to run without government interference. The idea is that if companies are allowed to operate unfettered, competition for shoppers will force prices down and quality up. Therefore, the government should not, for example, tell airline executives how to run their businesses or impose on food processors a lot of rules for packing foods to make sure they are safe.

In addition, Republicans also believe that the government ought not to side with the unions in their battles with business for higher wages and better working conditions. Democrats, on the other hand, believe that without such laws, the unions would not have a chance against powerful corporations, as indeed was the case in the past.

Some of the hardest fighting between Democrats and Republicans in the last four decades of the twentieth century was over social issues. Democratic party leaders, in general, supported a woman's right to end an unwanted pregnancy; Republicans generally wanted strict limits, and many wanted abortion outlawed altogether. Democrats also have tended to favor *affirmative action* programs, under which people who were discriminated against in the past and therefore were not doing as well as others, such as blacks and other minorities, needed to be given special advantages—for example, given preference in admission to college or in doing business with the government. Republicans have been more likely to oppose affirmative action programs, saying that it is up to each person to get ahead by hard work. It has been more common among Democrats to hold out for the widest possible freedom of speech, even if this allows the expression of obnoxious political views or the publication of what most people would consider filth. It has been more likely to find Republicans on the side of restrictions on pornographic expression in art, the press, music, and films. Thus we see in social matters, the roles are often reversed: Republicans want more government control and Democrats less.

We sometimes use the words *liberal* and *conservative*—or left and right—to describe these two main parties. These terms are emotionally charged, and furthermore, their meanings have changed over time. Take, for example, what we generally classify as affirmative action. The idea of such programs was extremely liberal in the 1950s, liberal in the early 1960s, and mainstream by 1968 when both Democratic and Republican presidential candidates endorsed them. Between 1960 and the early 1970s, the whole political spectrum moved to the left. With the election of the Democrat Jimmy Carter in 1976, the political ideas began to move back to the middle. The high point of government activism represented by the New Deal programs of the 1930s and all sorts of national government activities during World War II had passed. The New Deal programs like Social Security, banking, and stock market regulation, however, remained intact.

By no manner of means are all Democrats liberal, all Republicans conservative: many people in both parties are liberal on some issues, conservative on others. Confusing the matter even more, liberal and conservative philosophies are not altogether consistent: as we have seen, conservatives want more government control on abortion and pornography, less on the environment and business, the Democrats vice-versa. Yet the words liberal and conservative are so widely used today it is necessary that we understand them. Broadly speaking, then, the Democratic program as outlined above is termed liberal, the Republican one called conservative.

We will see, however, that over the period covered in this book, Americans have at one moment favored liberal policies, and other moments have been more conservative. But rarely has the pendulum swung very far in one direction before it is tugged back. The period we are looking at begins with such a swing of the pendulum. During the 1930s most Americans believed that an active government was needed to lift the country out of the Depression. During that time major government programs like Social Security, support for labor unions, restriction on banks and the stock market, and much else, were put through. Demand for war materials during World War II revived the economy and ended the Depression. (The Depression era is described in the volume in the series called *Progressivism, the Depression and the New Deal.*)

Franklin Roosevelt, president during most of the Depression and World War II, died in the spring of 1945. His vice-president, Harry S. Truman, took over. Nobody expected much of Truman, who had been for most of his career a relatively unimportant senator from Missouri. Even Truman was unsure of himself. He said that when he suddenly found himself president, "I felt like the moon, the stars, and all the planets had fallen on me." Truman had grown up on a farm, tried various occupations, including running a men's clothing store, and had gone on to study law at night, though he had never gone to college—the only twentieth-century president not to. In his early forties, he entered politics. He held several offices, and in 1934 was elected a senator. Roosevelt picked him as his vice-presidential candidate in 1944 as a compromise, when other better-known people proved controversial. When Truman took over he was seen as a man not really up to being president, but over time his reputation has grown, and by the late twentieth century many historians consider him one of the wisest presidents of the century. A plain man, he never pretended to be anything but what he was. "There was no pretense to him" one aide said. Another said, "He could talk to anyone. He could talk to the lowly peasant. He could talk to the King of England."

Harry Truman was essentially a liberal, who believed strongly that the government had a responsibility to aid those who needed help. His first problem, however, was to finish World War II and help settle the new world just arriving. He issued the order launching the first atomic bomb, which destroyed the Japanese city of Hiroshima and quickly caused Japan to surrender, ending the war. He has been much criticized for dropping the A-bomb, but among historians there is considerable feeling that the passions and politics of the time left him with no choice. (For fuller discussion of this controversial question see the volume in this series called *The United States in World War II.*)

But the end of the war brought with it other problems. In particular, there was the looming presence of communist Russia, that is, the Soviet Union. Before the war, almost all Americans had opposed communism, although especially during the Depression a tiny number believed that communism might be the answer to America's economic woes. During the war the United States and the Soviet Union were allies in the fight against Fascist Germany, and American hostility to the Soviet Union softened. By the end of the war large numbers of Americans felt that the Soviet Union could be a friend.

But very quickly old antagonisms surfaced. The Soviets, remembering American hostility of the time before the war, decided that they could not trust any of the western democracies. They quickly managed to dominate many smaller nations on their borders, such as Poland and Czechoslovakia, to compel them to adopt communist systems and to act as buffers

Harry S. Truman, standing between Joseph Stalin and British prime minister Winston Churchill at an important meeting at the end of World War II, was at first thought to be too unimpressive to be president. He soon showed that he could act decisively on the world stage.

Soviet troops in Czechoslovakia helped to keep the Czech government under Soviet control. Other nations along the Soviet border, like Poland and Hungary, were also controlled by the Soviet army.

against the Western European nations. In these nations they set up puppet governments controlled from Moscow.

Inevitably, Americans began to feel that the Soviet Union was bent on world domination—indeed, didn't communists believe that their system would eventually triumph everywhere? Truman soon adopted a policy of containment: the United States would not try to roll back communism where it already existed, for that would only lead to another world war; it would, however, act to keep it from spreading.

The Cold War between the United States, the Soviet Union, and their allies, was the central fact of the international world from 1946 to the collapse of Soviet communism in 1989. (It is discussed in the volume in this series called *The United States in the Cold War.*) Moreover, it would have a powerful impact on domestic politics. As we shall see, as the Soviet Union and the United States changed from friends to enemies, it became more and more risky for Americans to say anything good about communism, or even ideas which could be labeled "communistic." The effects on American society would be large.

Truman, while keeping one eye on the Soviet Union, also had to start putting the nation back on a peacetime basis. Obviously, the need for more tanks and fighter planes was largely gone. War related jobs would end. Would the Depression return? The problem turned out to be the reverse. During the war there had been no new cars made, no new refrigerators, no washing machines, or much else. People had made good wages working in war plants, and with not much to spend them on, had saved much of them. Now they began to splurge on all the things they had done without for years. Suddenly the danger was not depression, but *inflation*.

It is important to understand this term. Inflation occurs when prices and wages begin to spiral upward, chasing each other. That is, if prices rise, workers demand higher wages to buy what they need; as wages go up, things are more costly to produce and must be priced higher. Inflation does not hurt so much those who can get higher wages to meet the new high prices, but it does hurt—sometimes painfully—people with fixed incomes, like those living on pensions and insurance benefits, or others with set salaries, like school teachers and workers whose pay is set by long-term contracts. Some amount of inflation is considered almost inevitable, perhaps 2 or 3 percent, but when inflation gets up to 8 percent or 10 percent, as it did in the 1970s, there can be real problems for the nation.

During the two years immediately after the war, Americans suddenly saw inflation leap to 15 percent annually, which meant that after two years a savings account of $10,000 had lost about 30 percent of its buying power. It was in effect now worth only $7,000.

Many people demanded that the government "do something." Truman wanted to keep the price and wage controls that had been put in during the war, but Congress would only permit limited ones. It was a sign of a change in American opinion. The Depression was over; except for inflation, times were good. Americans no longer felt the need of the wartime regulations. The nation was turning from the government activism of the Depression and the war, to a more conservative laissez faire [hands off] mood. In the end, the Republicans would benefit.

The wage and price controls, although limited, helped to curb inflation. But workers in many industries felt that wages had not kept up with price rises. A wave of strikes swept the nation. Steel workers, meat packers, and many others walked off their jobs. By the beginning of 1946 900,000 workers were on strike.

Particularly critical was a strike of coal miners led by a fiery union leader named John L. Lewis. At the time coal, rather than oil, was the main fuel for trains, factories, and heat for homes and offices. A shortage of coal would have ruinous effects on the economy, possibly, some thought, triggering a new depression. Truman, as a Democrat, generally favored the unions over business, but he was afraid of damage to the economy. He threatened to put the coal mines under government control

Miners Granted Pensions

Sun-Telegraph

Strike Seen Ending; Lewis Faces Court

Workers, seeing prices rise rapidly in the postwar period, struck for higher wages to match. Truman, despite favoring the unions, took a firm stand against the strikes. Nonetheless, the workers often won much of what they had struck for, as did these coal miners.

and threatened to jail Lewis if the miners didn't go back to work. The strike ended. In a railway strike in 1946 Truman suggested that the government take over the railroads and draft the strikers into the army to force them to work. In time, the railroad workers got much of what they demanded. During the Korean War when a threatened strike could cripple the steel industry, Truman took over the factories citing his authority as commander-in-chief. But the Supreme Court declared his action unconstitutional, and a long strike followed.

The strikes and inflation of these years were hardly Truman's fault. Nonetheless, it seemed to many people that the country was in turmoil, and Truman got the blame. In the Congressional elections of 1946 the Republicans won heavily. For the first time since 1930 the Republicans had control of Congress. They quickly passed the so-called Taft-Hartley Bill which put some restrictions on unions' freedom to strike. It was only a mildly anti-union bill, but Truman vetoed it. Congress then re-passed it over his veto. The Conservative mood was growing stronger.

As the presidential elections of 1948 approached, Truman's popularity was down, and it was assumed that he could not win. Some Democrats even tried to persuade General Dwight Eisenhower, commander of the Allied Armies in Europe during World War II, to run as a Democrat, but he refused. At the Democratic nominating convention some southern delegates, who resented Truman's attempts to improve conditions for blacks in the South, walked out and started the States' Rights (often called the Dixiecrat) Party, with a southerner, Strom Thurmond, as presidential candidate. Many of the more ardent liberals were upset by Truman's hostility toward the Soviet Union. They, too, formed a splinter party, the Progressives, with Henry Wallace who had been vice president under Roosevelt from 1941 to 1945 as their candidate.

With Truman unpopular and many in his own party turning against him, it seemed clear that the Republicans could not lose. They nominated Thomas E. Dewey, a popular New York governor. Dewey felt he could lose only by saying

Thomas E. Dewey, shown here as governor of New York, was an efficient and intelligent administrator. Sure that he would win, he ran a careful, low-key campaign.

something seriously wrong, so he ran a very careful campaign, speaking mainly in platitudes nobody could object to. Truman, however, decided that the country's mood was not as conservative as many people thought. In one of the most dramatic presidential campaigns of the twentieth century, Truman swung around the country by train (there was little television at the time), attacking what he called the "do-nothing" Eightieth Congress, the anti-union Taft-Hartley Act that Congress had passed, and speaking against racial segregation in the South. He proved to be a great campaigner and won a close, but clear victory. The Democrats captured Congress, too.

Even journalists thought Truman had little chance of winning the election. This famous photograph shows Harry S. Truman holding up a copy of the Chicago Daily Tribune, *which went to press before all the votes had been counted.*

Truman now tried to push through liberal policies, but in fact even the Democratic Congress, dominated by southerners, turned out to be conservative in mood. It passed some of Truman's legislation, but turned down his plan for a national health program and various civil rights protections for blacks. However, Truman was able to start eliminating racial segrega-

The fighting in Korea was fierce. The troops were pitted against not only a tough, persistent foe but the terrible winter cold and snow of the mountains. Here, a soldier reads a letter from home. Americans were not always sure they ought to be fighting in Korea. During his election campaign Eisenhower promised he would go to Korea and seek peace.

tion in the military and the United States government, which he could do by presidential order. However, in June 1950 the Korean War began, and Truman had to turn his attention away from his domestic programs. (The Korean War is described in the Cold War volume in this series.)

By the election of 1952, Truman's popularity was sagging again. The Korean War was dragging on, costing thousands of American lives and tens of millions of dollars. The conservative trend continued. Truman saw the handwriting on the wall and decided against running again.

The Democrats nominated a moderately liberal governor of Illinois, Adlai Stevenson. The Republicans turned to the war hero, Dwight Eisenhower, and this time he agreed to run. He was a highly popular leader who fitted the country's conservative mood. The American people were weary of the war in Korea, a far-away place few had ever heard of before the fighting. Eisenhower campaigned as a "man of peace," and promised to go to Korea. He won easily.

Right-wing Republicans now hoped that Eisenhower would "roll back" the New Deal and abandon programs like publicly-owned power generators, government protection of labor unions, and regulation of banks. But they were disappointed; for the most part the major New Deal programs would stay in place. (Not until 1997 was one of them abandoned when Congress repealed the principal banking act.)

CHAPTER II

McCarthyism

It has sometimes happened in America that some liberals or conservatives push their ideas too far, to the point where they threaten American ideas of fairness and justice. This was the case with what has come to be called *McCarthyism*, when some conservative politicians tried to make it appear that every liberal idea was "communistic," and therefore "un-American," even traitorous.

President Eisenhower was not one of them. A decent and intelligent man, he was made very uneasy by the excesses of some of his conservative supporters. He was, however, a man who had grown up in a small town, Abilene, Kansas, and he had small-town ideals. In his boyhood many people lacked running water and electricity. Streets were unpaved, and grew thick with mud in rainy times. Almost everybody went to church and tried to be honest and respectable. People, they thought, ought to be responsible for themselves and not look to government for help. Eisenhower absorbed this conservative attitude in boyhood and it remained with him for life. As he rose in his military career, people respected him not just for his intelligence and ability to command, but because they trusted his sense of honor and decency. But given his conservative nature, it is not surprising that he was slow to confront the McCarthyites.

To understand McCarthyism, we need to realize that there had always been in the United States, and many nations elsewhere, people who held what are generally known as *left-wing* ideas and programs. There have been a great variety of such programs, but at bottom all want strong government control over business to prevent them, especially the large corporations, from exploiting their workers—underpaying them, overworking them, and forcing them to live in miserable conditions. Such conditions, unfortunately, had been the case in America in the 1800s and well into the 1900s.

Some of these left-wing programs were quite modest, asking only that workers earn enough to properly care for their families, that workplaces be safe, that products be sold for reasonable prices, and that people have reasonable medical care, retirement incomes, and a few other things. It is obvious that today the United States has put much of this into practice. But other left-wing schemes go much further. Communism, in particular, was built around the idea that the government, not entrepreneurs and investors, should own and operate all, or nearly all, businesses, which would then be managed by the government. As communism worked out in the Soviet Union, the government did indeed own and run not only industry, but also stores and services; the workers had little say in how the economy was managed. Instead, the workers themselves were completely controlled by a handful of people at the top of the government. Private property, the basis of the way we live in the United States, could be—and often was—taken by the government.

By 1950 Americans were coming to understand that communism, at least as practiced in Soviet Russia, was essentially dictatorial; in the matter of government control over people's lives it was little different from Hitler's fascism, which they had so recently helped to bring down. In time it came to be known that under Joseph Stalin millions of Russians had been murdered for opposing government plans. In 1949 a communist government came to power in China, and in 1950 communist North Korea, with Chinese and Russian support, invaded South Korea. Americans had good reason for disliking communism, and soon many were concluding that anyone who supported communism, or even found anything good in it, or any other form of socialism, was unpatriotic, even a traitor to the United States.

But there were those who wanted to press the matter further. Businessmen in particular feared and resented any kind of left-wing program, even the mildest ones, that threatened to interfere with their control of their companies or reduced their profits. They had a tendency, thus, to lump together all sorts of anti-business ideas as "socialistic," or even "communistic." From here it was a short step to concluding that any program that put limits on how businesses operated, such as limits on wages and hours, was unpatriotic. Many ordinary Americans, who disliked the

In this well-known, if somewhat romanticized, painting, the Russian leader Lenin is proclaiming the Soviet Republic. It was supposed to be a "dictatorship of the workers," but in fact it was under the total control of a few ruthless men at the top. The excesses of Communist dictatorships gave ordinary liberal ideas a bad name.

idea of "big government," agreed. Unscrupulous politicians found that they could gain votes by tarring their opponents with the stain of communism just because their opponents believed in this or that liberal policy.

These politicians were often able to play on fears of communism because during the Depression, many Americans had taken up left-wing ideas. Some had joined groups supporting such ideas, signed petitions in favor of them, written articles about them. Others had joined the Socialist Party, and a few, though only a tiny percentage, actually joined the Communist Party. It was not difficult to discover that this or that person had signed a petition or gone to a meeting in favor of some left-wing cause. An accusation of communism soon followed.

One of the first of the anti-communism crusaders was the Un-American Activities Committee of the U.S. House of Representatives. Dating back to the 1930s, the Committee, under the guise of rooting out Communists and "subversives" from government and elsewhere, mounted an attack on all sorts of liberal ideas. In 1947 they called before their committee some screenwriters from Hollywood who they suggested were promoting communism in their movies. Nothing was ever proved against them, but the so-called Hollywood Ten went to jail for contempt of Congress because they would not testify against their friends, and others had their careers ruined because movie producers, afraid of being tarred by the communist brush themselves, refused to hire them. The House Un-American Activities Committee investigated others, some of whom had once been Communists, some of whom never had; but the reputations of all suffered, and many lost their jobs and faced ruined careers.

Some Republicans now saw that they had an issue with which to flail the Democrats. They began recklessly hurling charges of communism in all directions. For one thing, they insisted that the Democrats under Truman had "lost" China to the Communists, because of supposed Communists in the State Department. In fact, in 1945 Truman had sent the much-admired General George C. Marshall to China to see what

The House Un-American Activities Committee, aware of the publicity value of movie stars, questioned many actors about their political beliefs and associations. Here, committee chairman J. Parnell Thomas, speaks to Robert Taylor, a movie star of the time, who named other actors as Communist supporters.

could be done about stopping the advance of communism there. Marshall had concluded that nothing could be done short of a full-scale war, which the American people would never have supported so soon after the end of World War II. By accusing Truman, Marshall, and the State Department in general of having "sold out" China to the Communist, these politicians thought they could gain votes for the Republican party.

One of those willing to use the issue of communism to gain votes was Richard Nixon. In 1946 he won an election by implying that his opponent supported communism, which was not true. He soon became a member of the House Un-American Activities Committee where he made a splash by accusing a State Department employee named Alger Hiss of spying for the Russians. (The charge was never proved, but Hiss went to jail because in the course of the investigation he lied under oath.) The Hiss case made Nixon famous and started him on the road to the White House.

A young congressman named Richard Nixon quickly seized on the issue of the "red menace" supposedly threatening America. With the publicity he gained he was soon thrust into the spotlight. In 1952 he became Dwight Eisenhower's candidate for vice president. Nixon and Eisenhower are seen here during the campaign.

The pressure to demonstrate a hard line against communism affected Democratic politicians as well as Republicans. The result of this was Democratic support, in 1950, of the McCarran Internal Security Act which required communist organizations to register with the government and publish lists of their members. Seventeen years later the McCarran Act was declared unconstitutional, but in the meantime it added to fears of communist plots. In 1951 Julius and Ethel Rosenberg were convicted of giving atomic secrets to the Soviet Union. Both were executed. By this time many Americans were convinced that the country was filled with Communists and other subversives, both in and out of government, who were bent on overthrowing the United States government. In fact, the number of outright Communists in the country was tiny, and the number of "fellow travelers," who sympathized with Communism, was not much larger.

But Democrats grew increasingly worried that voters might see them as "soft on Communism," as the phrase was. Truman, to show that he was not, had authorized a review of the loyalty of Federal workers in 1947. By 1951 two thousand people were forced out of their jobs, in most cases unfairly. No evidence of spying was found under this program, although as it later turned out there were, in fact, a handful of Communists in sensitive positions and a few of them were spies.

The stage was now set for the rise of Joe McCarthy, Senator from Wisconsin. He had grown up a poor boy in a small Wisconsin town and apparently still carried inside him resentments against people who were better off or higher up. He was a clever speechmaker and willing to say anything to gain favor with his audiences. He was also a very heavy drinker. In February 1950 he made a speech in which he claimed that he had the names of 205 people in the State Department "that were known to the Secretary of State as being members of the Communist Party and who nevertheless are still working and shaping the policy of the State Department." Although McCarthy never produced the list of names, or even a single name, newspaper editors, smelling a good story, front-paged McCarthy's charges. McCarthy, who had not expected his speech to get so much attention, decided to capitalize on the issue, and for the next four years in speech after speech he threw around reckless charges about Communists in government. He named few names and never produced any evidence, but proved very clever in ducking and dodging when people tried to pin him down. One reporter said that McCarthy couldn't "find a Communist in [Moscow's] Red Square." Nonetheless, people, seeing the damage that charges of communism could do, grew afraid of him. After awhile even many members of the press feared to attack him.

Privately many people, even some of his fellow Republicans, hated McCarthy and his supporters; Truman called them "animals." But it could be costly to fight him in public. Senator Millard Tydings of Maryland called McCarthy's charges "a hoax and a fraud . . . an attempt to inflame the American people with a wave of hysteria and fear. . . ." At the next election McCarthy accused Tydings of being a Communist. A faked photograph showing Tydings shaking hands with a well-known Communist was circulated. Tydings was a Democrat, but a fairly con-

Nobody was immune from charges of being "soft on Communism" or a Communist supporter. These women brought to Washington a petition that they claimed had thousands of signatures. The petition called for the removal from office of Dean Acheson, Harry S. Truman's secretary of state. Acheson, in fact, was strongly opposed to Communism, and was important in developing the American policy of "containing" it.

servative one. Nonetheless, he lost the election. Other politicians were soon following McCarthy's example. In Florida one Republican candidate said of his opponent that "Joe [Stalin] likes him and he likes Joe." It was typical of the times.

Dwight Eisenhower hated McCarthy and would privately rage against him and his tactics. Many people felt that if the much admired and immensely popular Eisenhower were to speak out, McCarthy's wings might be clipped. But Eisenhower was afraid that people would turn against him if he did so; he also wanted to let McCarthy ruin himself by continuing his outrageous charges. Even at the time many hoped that Ike would do more than he did.

But by 1954 McCarthy had made too many unproven charges too often. He over-stepped by attacking a man Eisenhower named as ambassador to Moscow. Republicans began to drift away from him. McCarthy started saying that the army was full of Communists. Congressional hearings on the subject were carried live on television, and for the first time millions of Americans saw McCarthy's reckless, bullying tactics at first hand. His support dwindled and the Senate censured him. In 1957 he died from the effects of alcoholism.

McCarthy was gone, but anti-communism continued to be an important strain on American politics for decades. In fact, there never was the slightest chance that Communists could take over the American government, or influence it in a real way. But many Americans continued to fear communism, and millions felt that the nation had a duty to fight it wherever it appeared. U.S. foreign policy was profoundly influenced by this extreme anti-

Senator Joseph McCarthy (left) with two of his young assistants, G. David Schine and Roy Cohn (right).

communism. Americans began automatically to see as enemies any nations, no matter how small, with communist governments, when hindsight has suggested that it might have been better to try to work with them.

Cuba presents a good example of this. A revolution there against an American-backed, but corrupt, dictatorship succeeded in 1959. Led by Fidel Castro, who aimed to undermine American control of the economy there, the victorious government became increasingly anti-American and took over millions of dollars worth of farms and factories owned by Americans. The United States withdrew first economic support and then official recognition. By the early 1960s Cuba was fully ensconced in the communist camp, and presenting a potential base for Soviet operations in Latin America. Indeed, the Russians built facilities for launching armed rockets into neighboring countries including the United States. Only a breathtaking standoff by President John F. Kennedy in 1962 brought about the removal of the missiles.

CHAPTER III

The Drama of the 1960s

The 1960s remain one of the most frequently written about periods of twentieth-century America. There were dreadful assassinations, the desperate war in Vietnam, and a dramatic shift in morality among the young. There is much to study. However, in this book we are focusing on American politics; readers interested in foreign affairs, such as the Vietnam War, the civil rights and women's movements, and the shift in morality, will find them discussed in more detail in the volumes in this series called *American Society in Ferment, 1945–2000*, and *The United States in the Cold War, 1945–1991*.

In 1960, the youthful, handsome, and dashing John F. Kennedy was elected president. Few American presidents have been so much admired as John Kennedy. Even at the turn of the century nearly forty years after his death, books about him continued to appear and the doings of his family made front page news. John Kennedy's father, Joe, decided that one of his sons would become president. A self-made millionaire, he used his wealth to buy political influence. When his oldest son died in World War II, the mantle fell to John, or Jack as his family called him.

Jack Kennedy had been a true hero in World War II, saving the lives of men under him when his little P.T. boat was wrecked in the Pacific fighting. With the help of his father's influence and money, he was elected to Congress. He married the beautiful aristocrat Jacqueline Bouvier, which added to his popularity. In 1960, after a tough fight, he gained the Democratic nomination for president.

Kennedy, though actually somewhat conservative in his opinions, took moderately liberal positions on issues like civil rights for blacks and help for the poor, in order to gain the support of the many liberals in the Democratic Party. The Republicans nominated Dwight Eisenhower's vice president, Richard Nixon, who had eight years of experience and press coverage. But Jack Kennedy carried an aura of youth and health—the Kennedy family was frequently photographed playing touch football and navigating sailboats.

The Kennedys were glamorous in their own right—good looking, wealthy, intelligent. When Jack married the elegant Jacqueline Bouvier it was icing on a beautiful cake. Two generations later the aura of glamour around Jack and Jackie remained strong.

It was clear that the election would be close. It featured the first presidential debate to be televised, and most historians believe that television proved to be crucial. Kennedy had recently been in California, was tanned and well rested. Nixon was ill, and had not rested for the debate. He did not permit the television people to put much make-up on his face, and he appeared as if he had not shaved. Under the hot lights he sweated a good deal. People who listened to the debate on radio thought Nixon had won, but those who saw the tired, sweating Nixon on television compared him to the vigorous Kennedy, and called Kennedy the winner.

A view of the first presidential debate, which was between Kennedy and Nixon. Although it is not apparent here, in camera close-ups Nixon appeared weary and unshaven, Kennedy fresh and vigorous.

It was immediately clear that henceforward television would be a major force in election campaigns, as indeed it has proved to be. Previously, presidential candidates were heavily dependent on party organizations to plan rallies for them, raise money, get out the vote. Now candidates, through skillful use of television, could reach millions of people without the help of party organizations. The parties became less powerful. However, there was a dark side to the power of television in political campaigns: television is very expensive, which means that politicians have to depend upon wealthy individuals and special interest organizations like business corporations and labor unions for money. In turn, such groups expected politicians to listen to their opinions after they were elected.

The Kennedy-Nixon contest proved to be one of the closest in American history. Nixon might have won had he appeared better on television since his platform differed little from Kennedy's. Both candidates said they would promote civil rights for blacks, develop a national health insurance program, and strengthen the military forces. Americans in 1960 clustered a bit to the liberal side of center, and Nixon as well as Kennedy sought to gain their votes. The two men left such strikingly different political legacies that it is hard to believe that voters had a difficult choice between what many saw as merely a pair of peas in a pod. Kennedy won with one of the smallest margins in history: 49.8 percent to 49.6 percent of the popular vote—a difference of about 120,000 out of 68.33 million votes cast.

Although John Kennedy had run on a platform of liberal policies, in particular helping blacks and the poor, eliminating slums and creating a national health insurance program, when he got into office he concentrated on the threat of communism. Many Republicans were still claiming that the Democrats had lost China, and were soft on communism. Kennedy was determined to avoid such charges.

Shortly after he was elected Kennedy had to deal with such a threat ninety miles from the American coast. As we have seen, Fidel Castro had allied himself with the communist Soviet Union. Many of Castro's opponents had fled to Florida and a few of them, with the help of the United States, were training for an invasion of Cuba. Kennedy had misgivings about the operation, but not wanting to appear soft, allowed what came to be called the Bay of Pigs operation to go ahead. It was a disastrous failure since the Cuban public did not rise up and support the invaders as had been forecast. Kennedy had more luck in facing down the Soviet Premier Nikita Khruschev when the Soviets began supplying Cuba with

nuclear weapons and missiles. In a death defying cold war game of chicken, Kennedy and the Soviet Premier locked wills over the Cuban missiles. Within days, after pausing at the brink of war, Khruschev and Kennedy came to an agreement: The Russians would remove the missiles from Cuba, and the United States would remove some missiles it had in Turkey facing the Soviet Union.

In another phase of the Cold War, Kennedy began building up

The Bay of Pigs fiasco was a disaster for all concerned. Here, a Cuban rebel leader, Alfredo Perez San Roman, stares gloomily from his prison cell in Cuba soon after the failure of the invasion.

military forces in Vietnam to try to prevent a Communist takeover there. (These stories are told in detail in the volume in this series called *The United States in the Cold War.*)

How the Kennedy presidency would have worked out we do not know, for in November 1963, John F. Kennedy was assassinated as he rode in a motorcade through Dallas, Texas, by an emotionally disturbed man named Lee Harvey Oswald. The Kennedy assassination has been the subject of scores of books, movies, articles, and television shows. Many Americans, perhaps the majority, believe that Oswald could not have acted alone, but must have been part of a conspiracy. Unbelievable as it may seem, two days after his arrest, as he was being transferred between prisons, another unbalanced man, Jack Ruby, was allowed to enter the Dallas jail. There in the presence of numerous law officers and on national television Ruby shot Oswald dead. Oswald never got to tell his story, and the obvious elements of conspiracy have never been confirmed.

Kennedy was succeeded by his vice president, Lyndon Baines Johnson. Johnson grew up in a middle-class family in the spare, poor cattle country of west Texas. He worked his way through a modest state teachers college and taught school for a year. He entered politics during the years of depression and Roosevelt's New Deal. By the 1950s he was a powerful figure in Congress, a man who through bargaining and arm-twisting could get bills passed. He and Kennedy did not like each other, but Kennedy had chosen him for his vice-presidential candidate in order to get southern votes. Johnson finished out Kennedy's term and in 1964 ran for the presidency himself. The Republicans nominated the honest and candid Barry Goldwater. Goldwater, however, was very conservative, believing that the Federal government should not subsidize farmers, provide welfare for the poor, or even aid education. And he was distinctly no friend of federal civil rights legislation. The great majority of American voters dislike extremes of liberalism or conservatism; Goldwater went too far for them. The national economy normally has a great effect on

Above: This photograph shows President Kennedy and his wife, Jackie, in the Dallas motorcade moments before he was shot.

Right: Lee Harvey Oswald, the man who shot Jack Kennedy, glares angrily at the photographer, as he is brought to the homicide bureau in Dallas for questioning. He, too, was soon killed by a man who knew some police officers and was permitted to get too close to Oswald.

politics, and in 1964 America was prosperous; voters do not like to chance a change. Johnson won in a landslide. He was the first man with a political career in any of the former Civil War Confederate states to be elected president since Zachary Taylor of Virginia in 1848.

Lyndon Johnson is mainly remembered as the president who most fiercely pushed the war in Vietnam, causing hundreds of thousands of unnecessary deaths. It is forgotten that, far more than Kennedy, he pushed through a great many important domestic programs. Because he needed the support of southern Democrats in Congress, Kennedy was slow to support programs protecting the civil rights of African Americans. But not long before his death he had presented Congress with a civil rights bill, which was meant finally to end most aspects of segregation in the South. Very quickly after Johnson took over he pushed a strong bill through Congress. This act outlawed discrimination on the basis of race, color, national origins, religion, or gender in public accommodations and employment, and gave the attorney general authority to use the courts to enforce its provisions. It also prohibited certain devices used in southern states to deny voting rights to blacks. In addition, the attorney general was authorized to bring suits against school districts to enforce the anti-segregation decision of the U.S. Supreme Court, *Brown* v. *Board of Education*, of 1954. Later Johnson introduced another bill to make sure blacks were allowed to vote.

In the 1964 election Johnson proposed to create a "Great Society" in the United States and soon set about doing it. He initiated a plan of federal aid to poorer schools; innovative because education had been almost exclusively a local concern. He persuaded Congress to institute both Medicare for the elderly and Medicaid for the poor, the first significant health insurance programs established by the Federal government. He set up a program of rent subsidies for low-income people. With the Water Quality Act and the Air Quality Act Johnson and Congress launched the first major Federal anti-pollution programs. Not since the days of the

Depression under the New Deal in the 1930s had Americans seen such an active Federal government reaching out to citizens everywhere. Not all of Johnson's Great Society programs worked; many of them failed. Nonetheless, President Johnson and a heavily Democratic and, therefore, cooperative Congress started many programs the nation by 2000 took for granted, like civil rights for African Americans, government medical insurance, and government protection of the environment.

But, Lyndon Johnson was, like presidents before and after him, determined to prove he too was not soft on communism. The causes of the Vietnam War are complex, but to put it briefly, after World War II, Vietnam had been divided into a Communist North Vietnam and an anti-Communist South Vietnam supported by the United States. Neither country was at all democratic, but the South Vietnam government was particularly corrupt. Soon Communists in the South rebelled, with help from North Vietnam. President Eisenhower sent military supplies to South Vietnam. Kennedy escalated involvement by sending in first military advisors, and then 16,000 actual fighting troops. Johnson, told by his military advisors that they could win the war if they had more men, kept increasing the number of American troops in Vietnam, until by 1967 there were a half million there. Nothing worked, and the death toll kept rising. By 1966 a growing number of Americans were speaking out against the war, including some in Congress. By 1968 a majority of Americans opposed the war. Among those most active in opposing the war were large numbers of students, who thought the war was wrong and did not want to be drafted to kill or be killed in such a cause. Johnson's popularity, despite the Great Society programs, plummeted. In March 1968 he announced he would not be a candidate for another term. But the damage done by his prosecution of the war in Vietnam could not be undone. It wounded the reputation of the United States a great deal around the world. At home, many Americans began to feel ashamed of their country.

Then, just as the 1968 presidential campaign was starting, and there

Lyndon Johnson was large in every sense, a man who drove aggressively to get things done his way. He accomplished much, but his determination to win the war in Vietnam eventually lost him the confidence of the American people.

seemed some hope that the Vietnam War could be ended, the much-admired African-American leader, Martin Luther King, Jr., was assassinated in Memphis, Tennessee, by a gunman named James Earl Ray. Eventually some evidence surfaced that Ray may have been hired by others to do the killing, but he died without naming anybody and the question remains unanswered. The King assassination triggered riots by blacks in cities around the country and further undermined Americans' confidence in their own government.

Lyndon Johnson wanted his vice-president, Hubert Humphrey, to get the Democratic nomination. But Humphrey had loyally defended Johnson's Vietnam policy, so there was growing support for Robert Kennedy, John Kennedy's brother, who was highly critical of Johnson's

The man on the balcony is standing about where Martin Luther King, Jr., was standing when he was murdered. The shot came from one of the houses in the background. In the courtyard below the balcony are reporters, police officials, and spectators.

handling of the war. Robert Kennedy, like Humphrey, also supported many of the Great Society programs that Democrats favored. Then in June he was shot by a disgruntled Palestinian angered by some pro-Israel comments Kennedy had made. Between the assassination of King and the two Kennedys, and the protests against the Vietnam War, it seemed to many that the country was falling into chaos.

With so much dissatisfaction on all sides, it is not surprising that the election of 1968 turned out to be very bitter. With the assassination of Robert Kennedy, Hubert Humphrey was certain to get the Democratic nomination. Although he was a liberal, his loyalty to Johnson on the Vietnam War turned many liberals against him in favor of Eugene

McCarthy, a former college teacher and poet, now a senator from Minnesota, who strongly opposed the war. Meanwhile the governor of Alabama, George Wallace, decided to enter the contest as an Independent. He was against black civil rights, and wanted segregation to continue. Many Southern whites decided to support him as did a surprising number of voters in northern states.

The Democratic convention was scheduled for Chicago in August. It was clear that Eugene McCarthy did not have the votes to get the nomination, which would go to Hubert Humphrey. Mayor Richard J. Daley, powerful political boss of Chicago and a strong Johnson supporter, knew that anti-war protesters planned to demonstrate during the convention. He alerted the police, and brought in thousands of soldiers and National Guardsmen besides. On the third day of the convention club-swinging policemen attacked peaceful demonstrators, in the process injuring reporters and innocent by-standers as well. A television camera caught the action, in which hundreds were hurt.

Eugene McCarthy, who was strongly opposed to the Vietnam War, was seen by many Americans as the candidate of the unruly students' movement. Just as they had rejected the very conservative Barry Goldwater, so too did they reject the very liberal McCarthy.

Police arrest a demonstrator near Democratic party headquarters during the national convention in Chicago in 1968. The demonstrator had climbed on a barricade and waved the flag of the Viet Cong, the rebels fighting the South Vietnamese and their American allies. Arrests of this kind were probably unconstitutional, but Chicago police had been ordered to stop all demonstrations.

A sign of the times is that most Americans sided with the police against the demonstrators, even though the evidence clearly indicated that the police, not the demonstrators, had started the riot. Nevertheless, the majority of Americans supported much that the demonstrators wanted, including an end to the Vietnam War and racial justice for blacks. But many of the demonstrators, especially the students, also favored the use of drugs and sexual freedom. They often deliberately and flamboyantly used profanity and obscenity to shock conventional Americans. Many of them believed that hard work and responsibility were out-moded ideals. It seemed to the majority of Americans, especially older ones, that these activists were trying to tear down the whole American way of life. In nominating Hubert Humphrey, Americans had once again shown that they would not support extremes.

Richard Nixon, who had lost the presidential race to Kennedy in 1960 and a race for the governorship of California in 1962, had seemed then to be finished in American politics. However, he was still a well-known figure. He had been quietly going around the country building alliances with important people in the Republican Party, especially among conservatives and "middle roaders." He seemed to offer stability and order and promised "peace with honor" in Vietnam. The Republicans had lost badly with an arch-conservative, Barry Goldwater, in 1964. They wanted somebody from the middle-of-the-road. Nixon got the Republican nomination.

It seemed at first that Nixon would win easily over Humphrey, who was burdened with the legacy of Vietnam. However, in time Humphrey abandoned his support of the war. The nation clearly yearned for order and stability, but there remained a strong liking for many of Johnson's Great Society programs, especially among blacks and the less-well-off who were benefiting from them. Like the elections of 1948 and 1960, this one turned out to be closer than anyone had expected: George Wallace received 13 percent of the votes and won five southern states. Nixon won by only 500,000 votes, a tiny percentage of all cast. But he did win, indicating that Americans wanted a return to stability more than they wanted social reforms. The backlash against the behavior of the student activists had, in the end, pushed many American voters in a more conservative direction.

The 1968 election changed the nature of American politics. The Republican Party had been formed just before the Civil War, mainly to end the spread of slavery. After the war Southerners saw Republicans as their enemy, and they became a "solid South" of Democratic voters. Beginning as early as 1948 as the Democratic Party became the party most associated with civil rights for blacks, southerners began to abandon it. By 1968 the efforts of Democrats like Kennedy and Johnson to end segregation in the South soured many southerners on the Democratic Party. Further, the more conservative Republican Party fit the southern mood. Increasingly thereafter the Southerners began to vote for Republicans or for southern third-party candidates.

At the same time, the Democratic Party was being torn between those who clung to the older liberalism of Roosevelt's New Deal, and those who wanted even more liberal, indeed radical, policies, such as the legalization of marijuana, the end to restrictions on pornographic literature, equal rights for women, and the de-criminalization of homosexual practices. The effects would be seen in the election of 1972.

CHAPTER IV

President Nixon and Watergate

Richard Nixon has proved to be one of the most fascinating, if devious, presidents the United States has ever had. He is the only president to have resigned his office in disgrace; and yet there is no doubt that he accomplished some important things, especially in foreign policy.

He was raised in Whittier, California, the son of a strict but loving mother and a frequently irate father. At many times the family was short of money and Nixon was forced to work very hard to help out. Perhaps he grew up resentful of more fortunate people. At any event he was driven by a quenchless thirst for achievement. Typically, he became president of both his high school and law school classes.

As he matured, he came more and more to believe that some people were out to get him and would stoop to any sort of unethical, even illegal, acts to do so. Therefore, Nixon reasoned, he would have to do the same. As a result he grew up to be something of a loner, a man never well-liked, but frequently respected for his shrewd intelligence and his ability to work hard to gain his goals.

He served in the navy during World War II and after the war was chosen by some conservative Republicans in California to run for Congress against a very liberal Democrat, whom Nixon suggested had communistic leanings. Just as the Democratic Party has always had its strong liberals and more moderate ones, so the Republican Party of Nixon's time was divided into conservative and moderate wings. Nixon himself was a moderate, but he proved adept at providing a bridge between the factions, which helped him in his standing with Republicans of all kinds. He developed into a supremely clever politician. He ran against another California liberal for the U.S. Senate in 1950, again tarring her with the brush of communism. He won, and in 1952 on the basis of his anti-communist activities, as we have seen, was picked to run as Eisenhower's vice-president in 1952. He then lost presidential and gubernatorial elections in 1960 and 1962.

Nixon came to office knowing that he had to get the United States out of Vietnam. He brought in as his National Security Adviser a Harvard professor, Henry Kissinger, also a shrewd, pragmatic man who believed that nations always did and should follow their self-interests regardless of morality. Nixon, however, like Kennedy and Johnson before him did not want to be known as the first American president to lose a war. He had promised the country "peace with honor." He and Kissinger worked out a plan for the *Vietnamization* of the war—that is, Americans would train the South Vietnam army, supply it with weapons, and gradually withdraw, leaving the fighting to the Vietnamese.

This could not be done overnight, and meanwhile the protests and clamor against the war continued. Many important people, including senators, intellectuals, and newspaper editors, were demanding that Americans leave Vietnam. Unfortunately, the suspicious President Nixon tended to take the protests personally. He felt that the protesters were not just against the war, but were against him, too. He started letting his aides try things that were unethical and sometimes illegal.

For example, in 1971 a former Defense Department official named

By the time Richard Nixon became president, the Vietnam War had become exceedingly unpopular, not merely with students, who might have to fight in it, but with the majority of Americans of all ages. Here, students gather near the Washington Monument during a large demonstration.

Daniel Ellsberg leaked to the *New York Times* a secret study of the Vietnam War by the Defense Department which showed that the government—under Johnson as well as Nixon—had not always told the American people the truth about the war. Some of Nixon's aides broke into the office of Ellsberg's psychiatrist, looking for information that could be used against Ellsberg. This, of course, was illegal.

Nixon and his assistants drew up a list of people they considered their enemies, mostly anti-Vietnam War protesters and political liberals, and tried to harass them, for example by checking their tax returns to see if they could find wrong-doing. Worse, soon after he became president,

Nixon worked out a secret plan to bomb North Vietnamese supply routes that went through neighboring Cambodia. The records of the bombings were falsified to make it seem that they were dropping their bombs in Vietnam, not Cambodia.

Nevertheless, right from the beginning Nixon began reducing the number of American troops in Vietnam, meanwhile trying to negotiate a peace treaty with North Vietnam that would give South Vietnam a chance to stand on its own. But he hedged his bet and began planning a new offensive which he hoped would force the North Vietnamese to give up the fight. In April 1970, he announced a plan to send ground troops into Cambodia, where the North Vietnamese had bases.

The reaction to this plan to expand the war into Cambodia was immediate and powerful, especially on college campuses. Hundreds of thousands of students demonstrated, and a hundred thousand people marched on Washington. In May at Kent State University in Ohio demonstrating students rioted on campus and in the nearby town and jeered at National Guardsmen brought on to the campus to control them. Some of the students began throwing stones. The guardsmen opened fire; four students were killed and nine wounded. Ten days later two black students were killed by police in a demonstration at Jackson State College in Mississippi. So strong was student reaction that some colleges closed down for the rest of the year. Nixon was forced to cancel the Cambodian invasion.

From that point on his aim was to gain a peace treaty. In 1971 he started a heavy bombing campaign in North Vietnam to push the North Vietnamese into agreeing to a treaty. Once again Nixon was heavily criticized. Finally, in 1973 a treaty was agreed to: the Americans would quickly withdraw, the North Vietnamese would not fight anymore. Everybody knew that they would fight, anyway, but Nixon hoped that the South Vietnam forces were now strong enough to defend their country.

By this time President Nixon was facing serious difficulties from

Ohio National Guardsmen were called out to stop an anti-war demonstration at Kent State University. Some guardsmen started to fire when demonstrators threw stones at them, and four students were killed. Here, medics wheel a stretcher in to pick up the body of a student.

another direction. In 1972 he faced an election. Nixon knew he was growing unpopular. There had been Cambodia, for one thing. For another, after two decades of almost continuous prosperity, the economy had begun to slide. Although that was not Nixon's fault, presidents usually get blame or credit for good and bad economic times. Another problem facing Nixon was what historians have called "divided government"— when Congress is controlled by one political party and the presidency by the other. This situation makes it extremely difficult to get anything done at all, and the president usually takes the blame.

Actually, Nixon need not have worried. Passions aroused by the Vietnam War protests, and incidents such as Kent State, had swung many Democrats behind the anti-war liberal senator George McGovern of South Dakota. This was especially true of younger activists, who were so sure that they were morally right they could not see any justice in opposing opinions. McGovern got the Democratic nomination. To millions of Americans he seemed to be the candidate of disorderly students, with their motto of "sex, drugs, and rock and roll." Polls showed that Nixon would easily win.

But he was determined to take no chances, and he allowed, even encouraged, his subordinates to engage in unethical and illegal tricks to make sure he won. In June 1972, police arrested five men who had broken into the offices of the Democratic National Committee in the Watergate office complex in Washington. Two young reporters for the *Washington Post,* Carl Bernstein and Robert Woodward, began to dig into what their editors at first thought was an unimportant story. They quickly discovered that some of the burglars had connections to the White House, indeed had worked for the president's staff. In January the burglars were put on trial. The presiding judge, John Sirica, sensed that there was more to the case than a simple robbery, and he pressed the burglars hard.

By now public interest in the case had been aroused. The Senate set up a special committee to investigate the whole matter. Soon one of the defendants agreed to talk to Judge Sirica and the Senate committee. The dam broke, and other defendants also agreed to talk. They revealed that several of Nixon's top aides, including his attorney general, the nation's top law officer, had been involved one way or another in the Watergate break-in. Soon the attorney general and other close aids resigned. Many of them were brought to trial. Six went to jail for their roles in Watergate, and others, including four of Nixon's cabinet members, were also convicted of similar crimes.

There was, however, no clear evidence that Nixon himself had been involved in Watergate, or had approved of it. There still is no firm evidence. But by 1973 it was becoming clear that Nixon had worked with his aides to cover up the Watergate story. Covering up a crime is called *obstruction of justice*, and is illegal. If Nixon had been involved in the cover up, he would be guilty of a serious crime.

As the Watergate case was blowing up around him, Nixon was suddenly faced with a problem from another quarter. His vice-president was Spiro Agnew, a former governor of Maryland. Witnesses were saying that Agnew had accepted bribes and kickbacks not just as governor, but as vice-president, too. The evidence was solid. Agnew was allowed to plead guilty to the lesser charge of evading his taxes, and to resign. Until this time a situation like this would have left the vice presidency vacant until the next presidential election. But not so in 1973. Ironically, back in the 1950s, when Nixon had been vice-president, Eisenhower had suffered a

Vice President Spiro Agnew was accused of taking bribes and "kick-backs" from contractors. At a press conference he expressed confidence in "complete vindication," but the evidence was too strong and he was allowed to resign without facing criminal charges. Nixon was already facing pressure to resign himself, and he picked Gerald Ford as his new vice president, knowing that Ford might well move into the White House.

serious, though brief, illness. Nixon had given some thought to the problem of succession—who would take over if both president and vice-president were dead or disabled. In 1967 a new succession law, the 25th Amendment to the Constitution, was ratified. This gave the president the power to choose, with the assent of a majority of both houses of Congress, a new vice-president when necessary.

Everybody knew that Nixon might be impeached, or forced to resign, because of Watergate, although when Agnew resigned impeachment or resignation were still only possibilities. Nevertheless, the man Nixon chose for vice-president might well become president. Nixon selected Gerald Ford, Republican leader of the House of Representatives. Ford was popular with other members of the House and with voters back in Michigan, but was not widely known across the country.

Meanwhile, the jaws of justice were closing around the President. He had been forced to appoint a special prosecutor to look into the Watergate matter. The Senate committee was still holding hearings. Still, nobody had come up with any solid evidence that Nixon had known anything about the burglary or had attempted to cover it up.

Then, almost accidentally, it came out that Nixon had installed in his office a secret tape machine that recorded conversations and phone calls there. Nixon's reason for putting in the tape machine was partly for the historical record, and partly so he could check on what people had told him, or agreed to in his office. It was for him a bad mistake. As soon as it was known that these tapes existed, both the prosecutor and the Senate committee demanded to hear them.

Nixon refused to give up the tapes, claiming *executive privilege*—that is, the right of the president to keep his conversations, papers, memos, confidential. Gradually, under public pressure, he began to turn over transcripts of some of the tapes. Nobody was satisfied; it appeared clear that Nixon was stalling. The issue went to the Supreme Court. The Court agreed that presidents must have a right to keep their papers and con-

The Watergate case blew wide open when Nixon aide John W. Dean III told the story to the Senate Watergate Committee. Here Dean, shown with his wife, waits to testify.

versations confidential: A president has to be free to consider unpopular ideas, to discuss political tactics, military and diplomatic secrets. But the Supreme Court added that executive privilege was not unlimited; when it came to potentially criminal court cases, especially when the president himself might be involved, he could not claim executive privilege. Nixon had to turn over the tapes. He did, and he was heard discussing ways to cover up the Watergate break-in. Very quickly impeachment proceedings were started. Nixon agonized over his decision; then, when it became clear that he would be impeached, he resigned, the only president ever to do so. Gerald Ford became president. Ford quickly appointed Nelson Rockefeller, former governor of New York for his vice-president. The country now had, for the first time ever, both president and vice-president who had not been elected to those offices.

The story of Richard Nixon has been seen by some people as a tragic one. Over the years since Watergate, evidence has come out that he was drinking too much, and using medical drugs to calm himself. At times he appears to not have been thinking sensibly.

We must remember, however, that Richard Nixon had some successes, especially in foreign affairs. His main triumph was to open official contact with Communist China, which, by the year 2000 led to increasing commercial ties with the United States, and some movement toward private capitalism in China. He was also the first American president to visit Moscow, and tried—unsuccessfully—to open talks with the Soviet Union on reducing atomic weapons. Though he depended heavily on his advisor, Henry Kissinger, in foreign policy, it was President Nixon who

Incoming President Gerald Ford and his wife escort the Nixons across the White House lawn to a waiting helicopter following Nixon's resignation as a result of the Watergate cover-up.

had the courage to take these steps. Nixon also signed into law a number of bills that had been initiated by the Democratic congress. Affirmative action programs for African-Americans, an environmental protection act, and the Occupational Safety and Health Act were put in place during Nixon's time in office. Thus Nixon learned to work with Congress during a period of "divided government."

CHAPTER V

The Pendulum
Swings Again

With Richard Nixon's resignation in August 1974, Gerald Ford became president. Within a month Ford gave Nixon an unconditional pardon for all Federal crimes he may have committed—Nixon has to this day never actually been proved guilty of any crimes, although the evidence that he was involved in the Watergate cover-up seems clear. Ford also allowed Nixon to keep the incriminating tapes, with the proviso that they could not be destroyed for three years in case a court wanted them. Nixon was to admit he had "made mistakes," but was not asked to confess guilt.

Ford explained that he did not want to drag the nation through a long and divisive trial. However, the public took it for granted that a deal had been made: Ford had been made vice-president in exchange for promising to pardon Nixon. There has never been any evidence of such a deal, but because of the pardon Ford's popularity dropped instantly and never quite recovered.

In any case, President Ford had problems enough as it was. In 1973, as Watergate was heating up, the Organization of Petroleum Exporting Countries (OPEC), most of them in the Mid-East, had cut back on the production of oil, and oil prices shot skyward. There were long lines at filling stations and the price of gasoline nearly doubled. Americans, used to cheap gas, were enraged. The sudden rise in gas prices, along with other factors, caused a sharp upsurge in inflation. Congress wanted to reduce taxes and increase Federal spending, tactics which many economists then thought, though inflationary, would help to keep the economy moving. Ford refused; for this, and other reasons, the nation fell into the worst recession it had seen since the great Depression of the 1930s. The great post-World War II prosperity was over. Many younger Americans, millions of them well into their thirties, could not remember hard times, and they were shocked. Unemployment reached 9 percent in 1975, the government was running a huge deficit, and New York City was on the verge of bankruptcy, from which the Federal government eventually saved it.

These financial problems were bad enough by themselves, but they contributed to another problem, which is difficult to pin down, but was equally serious. That was the damage done to American morale by the events of the years between the mid-1960s and mid-1970s. There had been the Vietnam war, which many Americans had hated, and which the nation finally lost. Younger people had been deeply distressed not only by Vietnam, but also by the problems of blacks and other minorities, and what they saw as an oppressive society determined to stop them from living as they wanted. Older Americans were appalled by the behavior of so many of the younger generation with their use of drugs, obscenity, and disregard for traditional morality. Everybody was disgusted by Watergate, and government lying about events in Vietnam. Most Americans, most of the time, had been proud of their country, which they had seen, quite rightly, as the freest and most prosperous nation in the world. By 1975 they could not be so proud of it.

We have seen how economic conditions often influence elections. President Ford was certainly not responsible for the upward spurt of oil prices nor the downward turn of the American economy. He did not do much to help, however, and in any case got the blame. By the time of the 1976 elections his popularity had collapsed. The Democratic challenger who emerged was the former governor of Georgia, Jimmy Carter. A navy officer in World War II, and an engineer, he had taken over his father's business of growing peanuts, cotton, and running warehouses. He went into politics and became Georgia's governor in 1971.

In the 1976 election Carter campaigned as a Washington outsider, who was untainted by Vietnam and the scandals of the previous few years. Many Americans no longer trusted the national government to govern well or even be honest with them; "Washington" seemed to be a hotbed of deal-making and insiders doing well at the expense of the taxpayers.

In addition, Jimmy Carter was part of a broad and powerful religious movement of so-called "born again Christians," which was sweeping America. Such people often had had a conversion experience which had swept them into a direct personal relationship with Jesus. Carter was one such person. By contrast, President Ford, who had pardoned Nixon, and had long been a Washington insider, seemed to be part of the old system. Both candidates reflected Americans' basic political centrism. Carter was hardly less conservative than Ford, and Ford was very much of a consensus seeking moderate. Both were "small government" men. Jimmy Carter won, although once again by a very small margin.

Now the problems that had defeated Ford began to defeat President Carter. He could not contain inflation, nor do anything about oil prices, to which OPEC gave another boost in 1979, again creating long lines at the gas pumps. In general, Carter was at heart a conservative, very much in favor of small government. Like many Americans, he believed that the government often tried to do much that didn't work, and ought to be kept small. Carter set in motion the *deregulation* of business, a process that would continue for at least twenty-five years. Carter, then, reflects a reaction against the governmental activism of the 1960s.

We must understand that during the Depression of the 1930s

President Jimmy Carter (left) with his predecessor, Gerald Ford, in the Oval Office in the White House. Neither Ford nor Carter was able to solve the economic problems facing the country, and both failed to be re-elected.

Americans demanded that the government "do something." One of the important things it did was to set up a lot of commissions to regulate the powerful large corporations, to make them play fair with their customers and employees. Businessmen had always resented such controls, and by 1976, when Americans were no longer looking to Washington to solve their problems, many had concluded that business would work better if the competitive free-enterprise system were left uncontrolled. Republicans agreed, of course, and with their support as well as that of

Democrats, Carter and Congress deregulated the airline, trucking, and oil business, for example, letting prices for airplane flights be determined by competition instead of by a government agency. They did not, however, "roll back" the primary New Deal programs; social security, banking regulation, and the rest.

But the country's economic problems overwhelmed Carter. By 1980 interest rates and inflation were at record highs. Making matters worse, in 1979 a mob of militants in Iran, protesting certain American policies toward their country, broke into the American embassy in Teheran and took fifty-three American diplomats and military personnel hostage. There was little the government could do, short of an outright war with Iran. Coming so soon after the American defeat in Vietnam, this new sign of American helplessness enraged Americans. Carter tried negotiations, which failed, and then authorized a quick helicopter strike into Iran to free the hostages by force. This, too, failed. (Carter finally managed to get the hostages released on the last day of his presidency.) President Carter's popularity, already low, dropped further. Although some Democrats wanted to replace him as their party's nominee in the 1980 elections, Carter got the nomination and ran again. But he had little chance to win, for he was up against a man who would prove to be one of the most popular American presidents of the twentieth century, Ronald Reagan.

Ronald Reagan was a small-town boy from the midwest who had come to Hollywood to find fame in the movies. He became a fairly well-known actor, although never a great star. After World War II, as president of the Screen Actors Guild, he fought communist influence. Already somewhat conservative, in the 1960s he acted as a spokesman for the corporate giant, General Electric, and became a fervent supporter of big business and a thorough conservative.

He got attention with a speech he gave scores of times all across the nation in the early 1960s in which he promoted a "small government," state rights conservatism. But his brand of conservatism was not yet pop-

Carter sent a rapid strike force into the desert to rescue the hostages held by Iranians, but a helicopter crashed into a transport plane, killing eight soldiers, and the mission had to be halted. The failure of this mission hurt Carter with voters.

ular, as a landslide vote against the very conservative Barry Goldwater in 1964 showed. However, by 1966, reaction against student protests and rapidly changing lifestyles among the "baby boom" generation were making many voters more conservative. Reagan was elected governor of California in 1966 and 1970; he tried, and failed, to get the Republican nomination for president in 1968 and 1976. But by 1980 the conservative tide was running strong in America. There was the new religious movement, which was staunchly conservative. Larger percentages of Americans were older, and more people were moving to the South and Southwest, both predominantly conservative regions. Perhaps most important, the student movements had tarnished liberals' ideas.

Although Ronald Reagan was born in the Mid-west, he adopted the western style when he moved to California. He enjoyed horses, riding, and ranching. Voters were attracted by his hearty good humor.

Reagan, a trained actor, presented a positive, confident, smiling face to the nation. He insisted that it "was morning in America." He would make the nation militarily strong again and "get the government off our backs." He won in an unexpected landslide in the Electoral College—489 to 49 for Carter. He brought with him a Republican Senate and a sufficiently conservative House, although Democratic, to let him put through his policies.

Ronald Reagan was not an especially thoughtful president, given to pondering ideas. He stuck to a few broad principles he had long held, and left his aides and Cabinet officers to work out the details. Basic to his thinking was the idea that the capitalist free-enterprise system ought to be allowed to run without government controls. Government should simply stay out of the way. In Reagan's view even anti-pollution laws and restrictions on corporate mergers were unnecessary interferences with business.

A number of other ideas sprung from this viewpoint. The first was that businesses and wealthy individuals, who were usually business people in the first place, ought not to be taxed too heavily. This was in line with the "trickle down" theory—in Reagan's day called "supply side economics"—which said that if businesses and the wealthy can pile up money, they could invest it in new factories, new businesses, which will provide more jobs and higher living levels for everyone. As a strong supporter of big business, President Reagan was determined to curb the power of labor unions. When the air controllers, who were government employees, went on strike, Reagan refused to negotiate, fired them, and brought in replacements. The strike, along with the air controllers' union, collapsed.

One more idea flowed from Reagan's belief in the free-enterprise system. That, of course, was that communism ought not merely to be contained, as American policy had been applied for thirty years; but if possible, communism should be destroyed. Reagan called the communist Soviet union an "evil empire," and when there appeared to be a communist take-over in the tiny Caribbean island of Grenada in 1983, he sent in American troops to stop it, which they did. He was also aggressive in stationing missiles in England and western Europe whence they could reach the Soviet Union.

Taken together, these ideas required Reagan to both cut taxes and build up the military substantially. As a conservative, he also did not want to run the country into further debt. He pushed through his tax cut, and massive increases for the military. Then, to balance the budget he proposed to cut back on social programs for the poor, like food stamps and subsidized housing. Many members of Congress hated to see the national debt rise, but so great was Reagan's popularity that they were afraid to vote against his programs. Social programs were not cut as much as Reagan wanted, however, and the government began to run huge deficits. Under Reagan they were always at least $100 billion a year.

During his administration the United States piled up more debt than it had in its entire history since 1789.

To stem the flood of debt, Congress then decided to raise Social Security taxes. The Social Security tax is levied on only part of your income, if it is large—the first $72,600 in 1999. Thus people earning more than that pay a smaller percentage of their income for social security taxes. It bears down harder, then, on low-income people than on high-income people. The final effect of Reagan's programs thus were (1) a huge increase in military spending; (2) a reduction in social programs; (3) a tax *increase* for middle- and low-income families and a tax *cut* for the wealthy; (4) an increase in the national debt of massive proportions.

President Reagan was not responsible for all this debt. Part of it was caused by programs begun back in the 1930s like Social Security and in the 1960s like Medicare, which could not be stopped. But much had to do with Reagan's insistence on large tax cuts along with large increases in military spending. Taken together, the net effect was to increase the already rising gap in wealth between the rich and the poor. The top fifth of Americans were four times richer than the bottom fifth when Reagan became president in 1981, but five times richer in 1990. In that year the poorest 20 percent of households owned 7 percent of household wealth while the richest 20 percent owned 44 percent. (One constant, however, is that the wealthiest were also those with the most education.)

The growing deficit and the wealth gap were primarily caused by President Reagan's insistence on the military build-up, the main purpose of which was to confront communism wherever it appeared. He began supporting forces in Nicaragua and El Salvador which appeared to be fighting communist groups. The *contras* in Nicaragua, who were trying to topple an anti-American government there, could not have existed without American support. These efforts cost hundreds of billions of dollars, expenditures that were often hidden from the American public, and even from most congressmen.

Ronald Reagan also proposed the building of an anti-missile shield, using lasers and satellites, which he believed could ward off incoming missiles. This Strategic Defense Initiative (SDI) was termed by its opponents "Star Wars." SDI was in fact banned by various anti-nuclear agreements with the Soviets, but Reagan, who at the moment was not interested in nuclear disarmament agreements, decided to try to develop it anyway. SDI never got very far under Reagan and even by 2000 had not been successfully tested.

This was the cheerful, optimistic Ronald Reagan that millions of Americans liked so much that they twice elected him to the presidency by large margins. Here, with his wife Nancy, he gives the thumbs up for an election victory.

As the election of 1984 approached, it appeared that Ronald Reagan could not be beaten. His confident, winning personality and actor's skill on television caused many voters to overlook problems like the growing budget deficits and questionable armed forays in Grenada and elsewhere. The Democrats nominated Walter Mondale, who had been Jimmy Carter's vice-president. Mondale selected a woman, Geraldine Ferraro, as his vice-presidential candidate, in hopes of scooping up women's votes, but the highly popular Reagan easily defeated him.

The shine, however, was beginning to wear off Reagan. Many people were uneasy about the soaring deficits. A minority were unhappy about his casual use of force in places like Grenada. And there was a growing sense that President Reagan, however cheerful and confident he always seemed, had not thoroughly mastered his job.

Reagan's opponent for the presidency in 1984 was Senator Walter Mondale. Behind in the polls, Mondale chose a woman, Geraldine Ferraro, as his vice presidential candidate, in hopes of drawing the women's vote. Nonetheless, millions of women preferred Reagan.

Then, in 1986 the so-called Iran-Contra scandal broke. It started to come out that some of Reagan's aides had concocted a scheme by which they sold arms to Iran, a nation with which the United States was not officially on friendly terms. The arms sales were illegal. The profits from the sale of these arms were being sent secretly to the anti-communist contras in Nicaragua. Congress had specifically prohibited aid to the Contras in 1982, and again in 1984. But Reagan was sure that Castro's Cuba was fermenting communist take-overs all through Central America. Reagan put his anti-communism ahead of his oath to see that the nation's laws were enforced, and encouraged these illegal transactions. Eventually

Reagan believed that the United States should be militarily strong, and he had a tendency to send in troops to solve problems. Here soldiers arrive in Honduras, which was used as a base by American forces supporting anti-Communist Contras in neighboring nations in Central America. American troops did not fight with the Contras but provided them with supplies and training.

Reagan's Secretary of Defense was indicted for his role in the Iran-Contra affair. Others were also charged. Reagan's aides in the government insisted that the President himself had known nothing about the Iran-Contra affair, so he was never indicted. There is, however, evidence that Reagan had not only known about it, but actually authorized it.

In the 1986 congressional election, the Democrats won back control of the Senate, and it appeared that they might have a good chance of

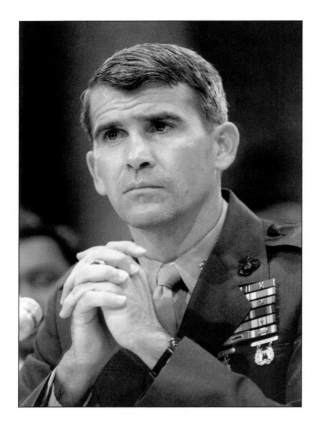

The Reagan administration cooked up an illegal deal to trade arms to the Iranians and use the money to aid the Contras in Nicaragua. When the story came out, it appeared that Marine Lt. Colonel Oliver North was a key figure in running the operation. Eventually it became clear that others, including President Reagan himself, were involved. Here, North testifies at the Congressional hearings on the Iran-Contra scandal.

electing a president in 1988. The Republicans nominated Reagan's vice-president, George Bush. The Democrats chose the relatively obscure Michael Dukakis, governor of Massachusetts, who seemed to have built a good deal of prosperity in his state. George Bush had never made much of a mark for himself as vice-president, and polls suggested that Dukakis would win easily. A recession that began with a collapse of the stock market which lost a record 22 percent in one October day in 1987 also damaged Bush's chances.

Bush attacked Dukakis hard, insisting that he was an extreme liberal, which was not the case. The Bush campaign was very negative: at one point the Republicans claimed that Dukakis had allowed a prisoner out of jail on furlough and that the prisoner had gone on to murder somebody. The murder story was true, but the furlough law had been put through by a Republican governor and Dukakis had nothing to do with any of it. Bush's television pictures of the murderer—a black man—suggested that Dukakis was somehow responsible: The ads were effective. In any case, Dukakis did not prove to be a strong campaigner, and Bush won handily. But the vote was more against Dukakis than it was for Bush; the Congress remained Democratic.

CHAPTER VI

The Middle Ground Triumphant

H istory is about the past. Most historians do not believe that they can make a fair assessment of events until considerable time has gone by—twenty years, surely, or more. It takes at least that long for us to see which events of an earlier day have important effects later on. Events that cause much excitement at the time often prove to be rapidly forgotten. We will, then, only sketch in briefly the last years of the twentieth century.

George Walker Bush was the son of a former United States senator from Connecticut. During World War II he was the youngest naval pilot to receive a Distinguished Flying Cross. After the war he moved to Texas and got into the oil business where fortunes were being made. He became wealthy and turned to politics, which he had grown up with. He was only partially successful, becoming a Representative, but twice failing to win election to the Senate. Through the 1970s he held various important government offices. In 1980 he campaigned for the Republican nomination for president. He lost to Reagan, but became Reagan's vice-president, and beat Michael Dukakis to become president in 1988.

The major event of Bush's presidency had nothing, really, to do with him. That was the collapse of communism in the Soviet Union in 1989. Suddenly, new democratic systems appeared there, and an effort was made, with support from the United States and other capitalist democracies, to introduce the free-enterprise system to Russia. These efforts were not always successful and by 2000 no one could be sure what direction Russia would take. However, captive nations, like Estonia, Poland, Hungary, and many others broke free of Russian control in the early 1990s. Many of these nations moved toward democracy and capitalism, some more quickly than others.

Some commentators believed that the collapse of the Soviet economy had been caused by Reagan's military build-up, which had forced the Soviets also to increase military spending, straining their economy to the breaking point. This was partly true. But the main cause of the collapse of the communist system was weaknesses in the scheme which had existed for decades. The Cold War, in any case, was over.

A second important event in the Bush presidency was the Persian Gulf War of 1990–1991. In 1990 Saddam Hussein, ruler of Iraq, invaded neighboring Kuwait. This small country had large oil reserves and had lent Hussein billions of dollars. By taking over Kuwait, Hussein would at once get hold of very valuable oil and eliminate the debt.

Kuwait bordered on Saudi Arabia, one of the greatest oil producing nations in the world. However, Iraq had a more formidable military machine. President Bush had spent his life in the oil business, and knew how important oil was to the American economy. He asked Congress for a declaration of war against Iraq, which Congress reluctantly passed. The Gulf War was short and was won by vastly superior American technology, which included "smart" bombs theoretically able to hit targets with pinpoint accuracy. (Actually, it turned out that American missiles were not as accurate as was claimed and did a lot of damage to civilians.) After five weeks of bombardment, but only one hundred hours of ground war, Hussein surrendered. The war cost 40,000 Iraqi military deaths and

As wars go, the Gulf War was nearly risk-free for the Americans: only a hand-ful died, compared with thousands of Iraqis. These American soldiers were hit by "friendly fire" from their own troops. One wounded soldier being evacuat-ed cries over the death of his buddy.

unknown numbers of civilian casualties. The United States lost 148 killed and 458 wounded, and her allies an additional 92 killed and 318 wound-ed.

Hussein was forced to allow United Nations inspectors to search Iraq for nuclear and biological weapons he was building. However, over the years the wily Hussein managed to foil most inspection attempts. The Gulf War did succeed in preventing Iraq from taking control of Kuwait and possibly Saudi Arabia, but it did not bring down Hussein or improve

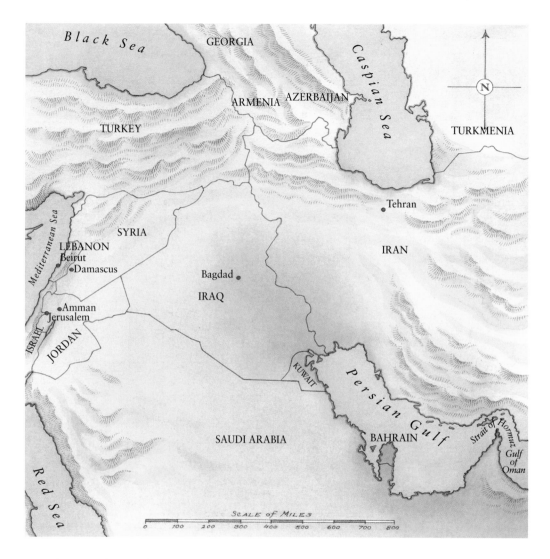

conditions for ordinary Iraqis. It did, however, put other potential aggressors on notice that the United States would move to protect its interests.

President Bush had less success domestically. He had campaigned on a slogan of "No new taxes," but when an economic recession rolled up in 1990–1992, the huge deficits piled up by the Reagan administration rose even higher. Bush was unable to borrow new funds to get the economy going again. The per capita national debt, which had been $4,338 when Reagan took office, and $11,545 when Bush became president, was $15,846 when he left office in 1993. In the end President Bush was forced to raise taxes, despite his promise. The voters blamed him for both the recession and the new taxes, which was unfair. His popularity, which had soared during the Gulf War, collapsed.

However, Bush's earlier high popularity had scared off many well-known Democrats from going after the 1992 Democratic nomination for the presidency in late 1991 and early 1992 when their decision had to be made. An obscure Arkansas governor, William Jefferson Clinton, stepped into the gap and won the nomination. Although beset by scandals involving women and shady financial deals (none of the latter were ever proved, despite great efforts by Clinton's enemies), he won with only 43 percent of the popular vote against Bush and a conservative third party candidate, Ross Perot, who drew the largest third party vote—19 percent—any candidate had earned since 1912.

Baptised William Jefferson Blythe, in politics he preferred to be called Bill. His father died in an automobile accident before he was born, and he took his step-father's name. He came to dislike this man but grew up with a mother he loved. Commentators have said he was driven primarily by a need to get people to like him. He was highly intelligent—even brilliant—earned a law degree, and became governor of Arkansas at the very early age of thirty-two. As a politician he knew that the American voter did not like political extremes. He aimed his policies at dead center, among other things taking over the Republicans' long-term preference for small government. As president he helped to cut down the number of people on welfare, and vigorously supported business, pushing through laws and treaties designed to make it easy for American businesses to compete in the new global economy, in which huge "multi-national" corporations, spread around the world, seemed

Bill Clinton, as he liked to be called, proved to be one of the most astute politicians of recent times. Despite many scandals, he continued to hold the admiration of millions of Americans for the warmth of his manner and his unquestioned intelligence.

to be outside the control of any single nation. All of these programs were favored by Republicans.

On the other hand, Clinton was a fairly strong supporter of efforts to control pollution, which Republicans considered an interference with business; he fought successfully to save affirmative action programs that conservatives attempted to abolish; and he worked hard to protect the environment, putting aside millions of acres of undeveloped land, a program bitterly fought by the oil, mining, timber, and ranching industries.

He also appointed more Hispanics, African-Americans, and women to high positions than any prior president.

Perhaps Clinton's most important legacy was the reduction of the annual deficit, even producing a surplus some years, which allowed the nation to start paying off the huge national debt. In part, of course, this was a matter of chance: during the Clinton presidency the nation enjoyed a record-breaking run of prosperous years, with the country's wealth increasing at an astonishing pace. Annual deficits that had reached $222 billion during the Bush administration disappeared as tax revenues increased and spending was held in check. By the late 1990s there were surpluses, which, inevitably, many people wanted to use to reduce taxes. Clinton insisted that paying down the national debt was more important than tax reduction. The majority of Americans agreed. This policy helped keep the economy strong, at least to the end of his administration in 2001. For most of his time in office Clinton was faced with a Republican Congress; he proved an astute politician who managed to hold the line against those who wanted to roll back affirmative action programs, environmental protections, and safety and health regulations in the workplace. In 1996 he was easily re-elected over Bush's vice-president, Robert Dole.

Clinton's time in the White House, however, was profoundly marred by a lack of good sense in his private life. He had always been the subject of rumors of extra-marital romantic affairs, and in 1998 he was caught in one with a twenty-four-year-old White House aide. In the course of an investigation about another matter, Clinton lied under oath about the affair. He always had a lot of enemies, and now they saw an opportunity to drive him out of the presidency. Impeachment procedures were initiated in the House of Representatives and Clinton was indicted for perjury and obstruction of justice. He then had to face a trial in the Senate. The Constitution permits the president's removal only for "Treason, Bribery, or other high Crimes and Misdemeanors." A majority of Senators did not

Scandals involving women tarnished Clinton's administration. Paula Jones was one of several women who claimed that Clinton had made improper advances to her.

think that Clinton's immorality constituted such a high level of crime and voted to acquit him. Nevertheless, this scandal which degraded the presidency and embarrassed the nation, undermined Clinton's effectiveness during the last two years of his administration and probably tarnished forever his historical reputation.

As we have seen, for most of the half century after World War II American politics had pendulated only between the moderate liberalism of presidents like Truman and Kennedy, the moderate conservatism of Eisenhower, and the less moderate conservatism of Reagan. With the Clinton administration the country appeared to settle at dead center. This was made even more apparent by the election of 2000, between the moderately liberal Al Gore and the conservative George W. Bush, former president Bush's son. It proved to be the closest presidential race in the nation's history, with Gore winning the most popular votes, more than a half million more than Bush who nonetheless won in the electoral college. On the day after the election, it turned out that many ballots in Florida, because of technical problems, had not been counted and became the focus of bitter disputes carried on in the federal and Florida courts, among politicians and the press. The balance in the electoral college was so close that Florida's electors would determine the presidency. As it happened the governor of Florida was George W. Bush's brother. Both sides appealed to state and federal courts to resolve the issue. Ultimately the U.S. Supreme Court (where two of the justices had been appointed by Bush's father), in a five to four decision gave the election to Bush.

The election of 2000 also ended with a Senate of fifty Republicans and fifty Democrats. The House was also closely divided, 221 to 211. (There were also two Independents and one vacancy.)

By the end of the twentieth century, then, the American public had made it clear that it did not like extremes of either liberal or conservative positions. They wanted governments that would provide them with certain programs they had come to believe they were entitled to, like good Social Security pensions, control of pollution to make the air clean, lakes and rivers safe for fish and swimmers, access to the best medical practices. At the same time, they wanted governments not to interfere with their freedoms. Americans still sought the middle of the political road.

In truth, to some extent the American people were trying to have it both ways. A case in point was the controversial subject of government medical insurance. Americans overwhelmingly wanted government to insure much of their medical bills and provide them with medical drugs at a low price. But they did not want these programs to cost too much, and they wanted to be free to choose their own doctors and have the best hospital care. Trying to find a way for the government to see that everybody got top quality medical care at low cost proved to be difficult indeed.

Thoughtful people saw other problems, too. Many believed that Americans had become too self-indulgent, spending too much time being

The Electoral College

The way we elect our presidents must seem strange to voters who first encounter it. It was constructed at the Constitutional Convention of 1787 as part of a series of compromises between state rights defenders and nationalists, southerners and northerners, and the promoters of the common man and aristocrats.

With a nation of fewer than a half a million voters spread out over distances that took three to six weeks to traverse, no telephone, telegraph, or even steam boats or steam engines, it was thought by the Framers that only a few active government leaders and politicians could know who best could serve in the office of president.

The idea was to use the states as voting districts, allowing each legislature to decide how the state's members of the electoral college would be chosen. Each state would have a number of electors—each of whom would cast two votes—equal to its number of Representatives, reflecting the proportional principle; and two more, as in the Senate, representing the idea of equality among the states.

The Framers assumed that only in rare circumstances would anyone receive a majority of the electors' votes, though a majority was attained in the first three elections. Then in 1800 a tie vote threw the election into the House of Representatives, as stipulated in the Constitution, where each state got one vote. This came about because the majority faction had unintentionally created a tie by casting each of their two votes for Thomas Jefferson and Aaron Burr. The political wrangling in the House ended with Jefferson's election, but in order to avoid a similar happenstance in the future, the electoral system was changed by the Twelfth Amendment to the Constitution. Now electors would vote separately for president and vice president, but still if no one received a majority the House would choose a president from among the highest three; and the Senate would choose a vice-president from the highest two in the running for that office. Congress has had to decide the election only once since 1800—in 1824.

entertained, instead of working with their children, doing volunteer jobs, seeing friends and family. Too much money, many thoughtful people said, was going into entertainment, and needless consumer goods, not enough into improving public education, modernizing railroads, protecting the environment. And it was obvious that the income gap loomed ever larger.

As these pictures show, by the end of the twentieth century ordinary Americans had access to a level of material wealth that was astonishing to the rest of the world. But some Americans believed that they were spending too much of their time and money on entertainment, and not enough on education, the environment, and other serious concerns.

Yet at the end of the twentieth century Americans had much to be thankful for. The country—at least superficially—was more prosperous than ever, although ups and downs were always inevitable. In general, the world seemed to be turning to democratic systems of government, although nobody could be certain that trend would inevitably continue. And the United States was, for the moment at least, the world's single

American prosperity remained the envy of the world. Here, some ten thousand immigrants become American citizens in a ceremony at the Orange Bowl. It was the largest swearing-in of citizens in American history.

"superpower." True, since World War II Europe had grown in strength and would someday present a challenge to America. Many believed that sooner or later China, with its enormous population, would eventually become a mighty force in the world. But in the year 2000 the United States was the only superpower and in addition had an economic and cultural impact greater than any other nation in the world.

Just after World War II some people had begun saying that the twentieth century would be the "American century." When the century was at last over, after its long, rocky course, it was clear that it had been.

BIBLIOGRAPHY

For Students:

Beschloss, Michael R. *Eisenhower: A Centennial Life*. New York: Harper Collins, 1990.

Cwiklik, Robert. *Bill Clinton: President of the 90s*. Brookfield, CT: Millbrook Press, 1997.

Eskow, Dennis. *Lyndon Baines Johnson*. New York: Franklin Watts, 1993.

Feinberg, Barbara Silberdick. *Watergate: Scandal in the Whitehouse*. New York: Franklin Watts, 1990.

Howard, Todd, ed. *William J. Clinton*. San Diego, CA: Greenhaven Press, 2000.

King, John. *The Gulf War*. New York: Dillon Press Macmillan, 1991.

Larsen, Rebecca. *Richard Nixon: Rise and Fall of a President*. New York: Franklin Watts, 1993.

Leavell, J. Perry, Jr. *Harry S. Truman*. New York: Chelsea House, 1988.

Selfridge, John W. *John F. Kennedy: Courage in Crisis*. New York: Fawcett Columbine, 1989.

Slavin, Ed. *Jimmy Carter*. New York: Chelsea House, 1989.

Sullivan, George. *George Bush*. New York: Julian Messner, 1989.

For Teachers

Ambrose, Stephen. *Eisenhower: A Centenary Assessment*. Baton Rouge: Louisiana University Press, 1995.

Burner, David. *John F. Kennedy and a New Generation*. Boston: Little, Brown and Company, 1988.

Caro, Robert. *The Years of Lyndon Johnson*. 2 vols. *Means of Ascent, The Path to Power*. New York: Alfred Knopf, 1982, 1990.

Ferrell, Robert H. *Harry S. Truman and the Modern American Presidency*. Boston: Little, Brown and Company, 1983.

Halberstam, David. *The Fifties*. New York: Villard Books, 1993.

Hargrove, Erwin. *Jimmy Carter as President: Leadership and the Politics of Public Good*. Baton Rouge: Louisiana State University Press, 1988.

Kutler, Stanley T. *The Wars of Watergate: The Last Crisis of Richard Nixon*. New York: Alfred A. Knopf, 1990.

Levy, Frank. *The New Dollars and Dreams: American Incomes in the Late 1990s*. New York: Russell Sage Foundation, 1998.

O'Neill, William. *American High: The Years of Confidence*. New York: Free Press, 1986.

Parmet, Herbert. *Richard Nixon and His America*. Boston: Little, Brown and Company, 1990.

Wills, Garry. *Reagan's America: Innocents at Home*. New York: Doubleday and Company, 1987.

Winkler, Allan M. *Modern America: The United States from World War II to the Present*. New York: Harper Collins, 1986.

INDEX

communism *(cont'd.)*
  Eastern Europe and, 14, **15**, 75
  fear of, 16, 25-26, 32
  hard line against, 26-31, 36-37, 41, 63,
    66-70
  Iran-Contra scandal and, 70
  liberal politics and, 24-25
  nature of, 16, 24
  politics and, 26-32, **30**, 49
  Republican Party and, 26-31, 36
  Soviet Union and, 14-16, 24-25, **25**, 75
  U.S. foreign policy and, 16, 31-32, 37,
    41, 66-70, **71**
conservative politics. *See also* extremist
    politics; liberal politics
  affirmative action and, 12, 58, 79
  of Carter, 61
  deficit and, 66
  Democratic Party and, 12-13, 20
  of Goldwater, 38
  governmental activism and, 13, 17,
    22-23
  of Kennedy, 34
  moderate form of, 22, 47, 49, 61, 81-82
  nature of, 12-13
  of Reagan, 63, 81
  religion and, 64
  Republican Party and, 12-13, 22, 47, 49
  shift toward, 13, 17-21, 46-47, 64-65
Constitution, 9, 55, 83
containment, 16, 66
contras, 68, 70
Cuba, 32, 37, **37**, 70

Daley, Richard J., 44
Dean, John W., **56**
deficit. *See* national debt
Democratic Party
  abortion and, 11-13
  affirmative action and, 12
  anti-war protests and, 44-45, **45**

  business and, 11, 63
  civil rights and, 19-20, 40, 47
  communism and, 26-30, 36
  conservative politics and, 12-13, 20
  deregulation and, 63
  divisions of, 10, 49
  dominance of, 9
  freedom of speech and, 12-13, 47
  gays and, 47
  governmental activism and, 10-11
  liberal politics and, 12-13, 20, 34, 47,
    49, 53
  political philosophy of, 10-13, 20
  social programs and, 10-13
  social reform and, 47
  South and, 46-47
  unions and, 11
  women and, 47
Depression, 13-14, 17, 26
deregulation, 61
Dewey, Thomas E., 19-20, **19**
distrust of government, 61
Dole, Robert, 80
drug use, 45, 47, 53
Dukakis, Michael, 72-74

Eastern Europe, 14, **15**, 75
economy. *See also* prosperity
  decline of, 52, 60, 77-78
  inflation and, 16, 60
  oil and, 75
  political impact of, 60, 63, 78
  strikes and, 17
  theories of, 11, 66
  after World War II, 16-18
Eisenhower, Dwight, 19-23, **28**, 30-31, 41, 81
election
  of 1946, 18
  of 1948, 19-20, **20**
  of 1952, 21
  of 1960, 34-36, **35**

JAMES LINCOLN COLLIER is the author of a number of books both for adults and for young people, including the social history *The Rise of Selfishness in America*. He is also noted for his biographies and historical studies in the field of jazz. Together with his brother, Christopher Collier, he has written a series of award-winning historical novels for children widely used in schools, including the Newbery Honor classic, *My Brother Sam Is Dead*. A graduate of Hamilton College, he lives with his wife in New York City.

CHRISTOPHER COLLIER grew up in Fairfield County, Connecticut and attended public schools there. He graduated from Clark University in Worcester, Massachusetts and earned M.A. and Ph.D. degrees at Columbia University in New York City. After service in the Army and teaching in secondary schools for several years, Mr. Collier began teaching college in 1961. He is now Professor of History at the University of Connecticut and Connecticut State Historian. Mr. Collier has published many scholarly and popular books and articles about Connecticut and American history. With his brother, James, he is the author of nine historical novels for young adults, the best known of which is *My Brother Sam Is Dead*. He lives with his wife Bonnie, a librarian, in Orange, Connecticut.

DATE DUE

DATE DUE

973.92
COL
Collier, Christopher, 1930-
The Middle road

973.92 CO
Hogg Middle School

3053068000029
The middle road